The **Perfect Pause**

The **Perfect Pause**

Meditating Your Way
to the Ultimate You

Eric Vance Walton

The Perfect Pause
Meditating Your Way to the Ultimate You

First Edition

Copyright © 2017 by Eric Vance Walton

ISBN-13: 978-1547082957

Cover and book designed by LuCe, luboshcech.com
Cover photo by Jonatan Pie
Mandala Illustration by Ruth Frances Greenberg, ruthfrancesgreenberg.com

To order additional copies of this book please visit: EricVanceWalton.net

"You must be the change you wish to see in the world."

~ MAHATMA GHANDI

For you P.Y.

Contents

The Edge of Understanding

this lonely road unfolds you,
quells the guilt that scolds you
and dulls the fear that holds you
in the place you stand today

then the veil is slowly lifted,
and wicked lies are sifted
once muddled thoughts seem gifted what is there left to find?

once precious ties are severed true
an epiphany, you forever knew
you no longer worry what you'd do….if
the moment's come and gone

so beautiful, this existence
when pure truth spans the distance
a call that makes maya whence
rings out from heart to mind

until now you've failed to see
that you're everything you need to be
won't you close your eyes and
walk with me out to the very edge.

Nothing Else Matters

As the sun's rays
illuminate your being
and warm your face
pause to take a nice
long drink of life,
close your eyes and smile.

Know that this moment
in time is real and
all there is,
really all there ever was
and will be,
nothing else matters.

People will feel how they feel
and will believe
what they want to believe
our only job is to be

Fall leaves will continue
their dance in the crisp wind,
the squirrels will continue to play
and the woodsmoke will wisp
long after we're gone

but now, there is the sun
and the Earth beneath our feet
and our breath. Time is still
and nothing else matters.

~ ERIC VANCE WALTON

A Note from the Author

Tread Lightly, Love Deeply. This is a philosophy that took me over twenty years meditating, living and learning to perfect. What does the Tread Lightly, Love Deeply philosophy mean to me?

Tread Lightly means leaving a smaller footprint on our planet and learning to live more in harmony with nature. Treading lightly means to connect with and be more mindful of the very ecosystem that gives us life every second of our physical existence.

Love Deeply means living both passionately and compassionately. It means to open your heart to the possibility of miracles and to believe that the realization of your dreams are possible. Loving deeply means learning to truly love yourself and the life you live. It also means to be more kind to our fellow man and have more empathy for those around us.

Prologue

I discovered the power of meditation at an extremely low point in my life. I was overweight, not exercising, and living a very unhealthy lifestyle. At my worst I was barely functioning. I struggled to leave the house for fear of crippling panic attacks. After a while it felt as though I wasn't even living. I was no longer in control of my life and I absolutely hated that feeling. The worst part of this for me was the shame. I knew I had more potential and that I wasn't living my best life and that feeling of limitation frustrated me.

The fear of the anxiety caused me to construct my entire life around a routine that kept me feeling safe and secure. As a temporary escape from my misery, each weekend I would force myself to get out of the house and would drive to a local bookstore. I spent hours reading about anything that interested me. One afternoon a tiny blue meditation book called, "Metaphysical Meditations" caught my eye so I brought it home, read it, and began to meditate. I then read Autobiography of a Yogi by Paramahansa Yogananada, these two books were the spark that began to transform my life.

After a few months of practicing meditation something miraculous began to happen. I began to notice that I was starting to slowly heal from the inside out. I felt more relaxed, I began to eat healthier, had better concentration, and was flooded with a general sense of well-being.

In 1991, about a year after I started my regular practice, I enrolled in a three year course in advanced meditation. I was so excited about the benefits I experienced through my practice I began to believe that meditation had the power to change our entire world for the better, one person at a time. At that moment I vowed to one day teach others.

Only in the past year, more than twenty years after I first began, do I feel even remotely qualified enough to teach and share this life-changing practice of meditation with others. My goal was to fill this book only with honest, simple, and actionable methods and concepts that have worked for me personally.

Getting to know your true self through meditation takes courage and it takes work. Each meditation session is like charging your cell phone battery. If you'd don't meditate just a few minutes every day the benefits you receive will soon be depleted and you'll be back at the same place you started.

Life in this world will never be perfect but despite what unfolds around us but you will learn through your practice that it's nearly always possible to remain peaceful, hopeful, and happy. The negative moods of those around you don't have to spill over into your own consciousness. You don't have to impose any limits on your life due to fear, anxiety or anything else.

At the end of most chapters there is a section called, "Put It Into Practice", these are simple ways to incorporate the methods presented in the book in your own life. Also at the end of each chapter you'll find a Notes page to jot down thoughts and ideas. If you're reading the eBook version of The Perfect Pause on a mobile phone or tablet simply place your finger on the Notes page and "long press" your screen to activate the Notes feature in the Kindle app. Use this notes feature to document your observations and results.

I'm convinced that this simple practice has the potential to heal the world one person at a time. As I sit here today putting the finishing touches on this book I'm reflecting on how completely my life has been transformed by this true miracle. Meditation is the greatest gift you can give yourself. Practicing it is the greatest gift you can give to the world. No matter where your life stands today, it's never too late to begin your practice.

Each year more and more people are waking up to the fact that this life is an incredible gift. Life gives us the opportunity to learn, to love, and to grow beyond our wildest imaginations. When you began to treat life as the gift that it is an amazing new reality will open up to you. It's a world that you may've only seen small glimpses of before. Meditation is your chance to join the ranks of the awakened.

Whether you currently realize it or not, you are miraculous, you deserve love, you deserve a life of happiness and fulfillment, above all you deserve to be the best version of yourself. Remember this now and for the rest of your days.

The Greatest of Secrets

You languish, awash in worry
that time is slipping by
and all that once was
has long gone down the road
never to pass your way again

they tell you you're a sinner
and you remember
when your innocence
wouldn't allow you to believe
but time and their wicked words
have so deliberately whittled you away

it is they who tell you to keep coming back,
dangling the hope of salvation
just beyond your fervor's grasp.

But there are a few things
that they have failed to tell you
you are miraculous, you are divinity's spark
the power of your soul is a sleeping giant, long exiled

if you only knew the power that you possess
your eyes would stream tears of joy as if awakened
from a terrible nightmare to realize the greatest of secrets...
you are an emperor
in beggars clothes indeed.

Namaste (which means: I bow to the Divine in you.)

A Special Request

Please do me a favor, if you read this book and put its concepts into practice, take a few moments to write a review on Amazon and share your experiences with others. Whether you loved the book or decided it just wasn't for you, I urge you to be completely honest when writing the review.

Also, if you know of someone who might benefit from the book, please share it. I don't care if you pass along your copy, this isn't only about book sales for me it's about my wish to make a positive impact in the world we share.

Please visit my Facebook page (www.facebook.com/EricVanceWaltonAuthor) and my website (www.EricVanceWalton.net) and sign up for my mailing list to receive exclusive offers and content only available to my newsletter subscribers.

Chapter One

Meditation is Liberation

You may have been drawn to meditation for a variety of reasons: to reduce stress; to heal from anxiety or depression; increase productivity; or just create a better life for yourself. The beauty of meditation is even if you begin your practice for a specific reason you will quickly start to experience unforeseen benefits in all areas of your life. What I've learned is meditation has the uncanny ability of seeking out exactly what is broken or unbalanced within you and fixing it. This allows you to become the best version of yourself, the greatest gift you could give the world.

The series of events that led me to meditation began when I was in my early twenties. My diet was bad, I wasn't exercising, and I was making poor life choices until eventually, a terrible depression set in. I was going to college at that time and ended up dropping out rather than subject myself to the embarrassment of panic attacks during presentations or class discussions. The panic attacks grew to be so random and so severe that I eventually stopped socializing and became afraid to leave the house. This crippling limitation that appeared to come into my life so suddenly baffled and angered me.

In hindsight I understand that anxiety and depression actually took root in my psyche over several years. Each time I backed away from a fear and didn't stand up to it the fear got a little worse and gained a little more power over me until the point it had full control.

One summer night, in the middle of a deep sleep, I had an experience that forever changed my life. At the time the extraordinary experience left me with more questions than it did answers. Over twenty years later I'm just beginning to understand it. Although I'm not ready to share the full details of this experience yet I can say that I'm sure it was the catalyst that led me to this spiritual path. It was terrifyingly transformative, consciousness-expanding, and in hindsight very sacred. Afterwords I developed an intense curiosity for all things spiritual and an unwavering desire to fight against anything that was holding me back from living my best life.

In the following months I spent countless hours reading self help books, some of which were slightly beneficial but only provided a temporary fix. After a few months of searching I was drawn to a small book on meditation in a local bookstore and it changed my life. I developed a regular meditation practice and stuck to it faithfully every day, even if it was only fifteen minutes.

Soon and idea came to me. I began to desensitize myself to the panic attacks by purposely putting myself into situations that I feared would trigger the anxiety and panic. Each time I did this I became stronger and the anxiety and panic attacks became less severe until they eventually subsided and I started to get my life back.

What I quickly learned is meditation is the best way to liberate you from whatever barriers are keeping you from being the absolute best version of yourself. We have simply forgotten how awesomely powerful we really are. Through the gift of imagination and the intelligence to bring our ideas to fruition, there is literally nothing in this world that we can't accomplish. Ask yourself, what would you attempt in life if you knew, in your heart, that you could accomplish anything? How would you live each day of the rest of your life if you had no fear of failure?

The sad truth is many people in life come close to achieving their true potential. One reason is that there are many external roadblocks that prevent us from relearning how powerful we really are. But none of these external barriers can compare to the damage we inflict on ourselves, often subconsciously, through negative self talk. Most of us are truly our own worst enemies when it comes to living the life of our dreams. Meditation will quickly make you aware of the quality of your inner thoughts and how they impact you.

As you begin a daily meditation practice you will also start to notice that you are so powerful that your own inner thoughts and expectations are creating your reality in nearly every moment. If you constantly dwell on negative thoughts you will have a horrible day. Think good, positive thoughts, and despite what life throws at you, it is easier to find your calm center and work through the challenges more quickly and easily. Perception is so vital to our happiness and success that I'm devoting an entire chapter to it later in the book.

Before I found meditation, negative self talk looped in my head almost constantly. By continually thinking negative internal thoughts and constantly comparing ourselves to others, many of us fall into a rut of sabotaging the quality our own life experience.

"I'm not smart enough", "I'm not as good looking or successful as they are", "This certain person doesn't like me", "This idea will never work." Sound familiar?

Marianne Williamson said, *"Our deepest fear is not that we are inadequate. Our deepest fear is that we are powerful beyond measure. It is our light, not our darkness, that most frightens us. We ask ourselves, who am I to be brilliant, gorgeous, talented, and fabulous? Actually, who are you not to be?"*

This quote is important because I've come to realize that subconsciously most of us know exactly how powerful we are and it terrifies us. Why? If we admit that we have the power to transform ourselves and accomplish anything in life it's impossible to blame anyone or anything else for our own unhappiness. Think about this for a moment.

Most of us have heard of the word, "institutionalized" and know its meaning but few of us realize that we have become institutionalized ourselves. Nothing illustrates this concept better than my favorite film, "A Shawshank Redemption." As unbelievable as it seems, it is common for prisoners who have been incarcerated for decades, when released, to find themselves unable to deal with freedom. Freedom terrifies them. Some even end up breaking the law to get back into prison. These people, who at first grieve because their freedom has been taken from them, strangely begin to find security and comfort behind the bars that keep them in bondage.

The same phenomena occurs in our daily lives. When we're young, most of us have clear dreams and aspirations but if we're not mindful, as the ocean erodes the sand, the routines of life slowly wear our dreams away. After a few years our dreams are pushed back into the farthest corners of our minds and are likely labeled as naive illusions.

As our daily routines literally become etched onto our brains, even though we may be miserably unhappy in our lives, we lose our ability to even imagine a different way of living. We become so dependent upon the routine itself that we forget that other options that would make us far happier exist and are just a decision away!

As you will experience, meditation is many wonderful things but first and foremost it is a process of relearning who we really are and unleashing the awesome power that each and every one of us possess. We are like sleeping giants that merely have to be awakened.

PUTTING IT INTO PRACTICE

Take a moment to access your strengths and weaknesses. What are you really good at? What things about yourself would you like to improve? What are your personal and professional goals for the next year?

List the answers to these questions in the Notes page at the end of this chapter. After a few months of meditation practice, revisit these notes and use them as a guide to see how far you've progressed in your development.

NOTES

— Fast learner,
— I love that I'm neat
— Better at over coming
  most of my past fears
— More outgoing than I used to be
  — Still shy (could work on bettering
    social skills)
— Negative thinker (always thinking
  about the worst out comes or
  scenarios)

Goals

* NO MORE DWI's *
  — stay out of trouble with the law
  — Go to school (find some thing you're
    really passionate about / or good at)
  — less partying (less drinking)
  — Save HELLA $

NOTES

NOTES

NOTES

NOTES

NOTES

Chapter Two

Three Steps

Modern life is like a double-edged sword. Although the average person enjoys a reasonable amount of leisure time, it doesn't feel that way. Thanks to our mobile phones, we have instant access to more information than any other generation in history but we also have countless distractions. Our senses are assaulted from the time our alarm clocks wake us in the morning to the time we drift off to sleep at night. In addition to mobile phones there's also television, radio, billboards and numerous others things competing for our attention constantly.

All of these distractions and demands make the first step of meditation the biggest challenge. The first step is what I refer to as the Physical Step and requires us to calm our bodies and quiet our minds. This must happen before we can reestablish the connection to our souls and to the universe.

The act of meditation is like connecting our souls to a deep unfathomable knowledge that is available to everyone and everything. This is very similar to the way your mobile phone connects to the internet through Wi-fi or a cellular signal. For you to establish this vital connection you must first be able to attain a certain level of peace within yourself.

Once the mind is still the second phase, the Psychological Step, begins. This is when we start to release the baggage that we've acquired throughout the years. Psychological scars will begin to heal, you will feel as though you are putting the past behind you, and you will feel a sense of completeness. In this second phase our perspectives begin to shift ever so slightly. We start to gradually break free from negativity, self-limiting thoughts, and behaviors that have become a destructive habits in our lives.

The third and final step of meditation is the Spiritual Step. This is deep meditation and words cannot fully describe what will happen. I can only tell you it will change your life for the better. You will regain the power to be the best version of yourself each day for the rest of your life.

The beautiful thing about meditation is you don't have to understand the mechanics of how it's working. The only thing required of you is have the faith and resolve to practice. If you make an effort to meditate, even fifteen minutes a day, incredible transformation and healing will happen on its own. If you make meditation part of your routine, the deep knowledge that you're connecting with in your practice will do all the work. It will trigger a threefold healing process: physical, psychological, and spiritual. It's never a bad time or too late to start your practice. Whatever challenges you're struggling with, meditation will help get you quickly on the road to a better you.

To paraphrase Sir Isaac Newton's first law of motion, "The natural state of an object is to be at rest." I believe that the natural state of our souls is to be at rest. When we calm our desires, fears, and anxieties through meditation, again our souls are at rest. When we achieve this state we feel well-being, peace, and joy. We feel as though we've come home. We've all felt fleeting and maybe even extended moments of true happiness where it seems a light is radiating from the inside out and nothing can go wrong. What if I told you it was possible to feel this way more often than not?

Each of us, whether we're conscious of it or not, are living our lives in a desperate attempt to find a way back to that perfect state of joy. Unfortunately, many people choose harmful paths to achieving that peaceful state like ingesting mood altering substances, chasing adrenaline-inducing thrills, seeking approval or praise from others, working too much, overeating, or spending beyond their means. All of these things are merely temporary triggers that release a flood of the naturally occurring "happiness chemicals" in our brains including endorphins, dopamine, serotonin, and oxycontin. The trouble is most of these triggers are unhealthy and eventually lead to a downward spiral of addiction and misery.

Meditation will provide a better outcome with no harmful side effects. It truly is the "perfect pause", the one true path back to our soul's natural state of rest, and our perfect state of happiness. In the coming chapters I offer you a way to return to your natural state. Side effects may include: sound sleep, lower blood pressure, increased productivity, better focus and memory, longer attention span, decreased anxiety, more creativity, and increased compassion.

PUTTING IT INTO PRACTICE

Like an anchor, our breath is what tethers our soul to this physical world. How you breathe will tell you a lot about your current physical and mental state. *Are you breathing rapid, shallow breathes or slow, deep breaths?*

Take a moment right now to pay attention to the quality of your breathing. Proper breathing requires full expansion of the lower lobes of your lungs. Your belly (not just your chest) should rise and fall with each inhalation and exhalation.

Spend the next few minutes breathing properly, making sure your belly rises and falls. Afterwards, use the Notes section found at the end of this chapter to document how you were breathing before and how you felt after a few minutes of slower, deeper breathing.

Set a reoccurring reminder on your mobile phone to notify you a couple times per day with just the word "breathe." When you see the notification, think about the quality of your breath and make a conscious effort to breathe more slowly and deeply. Over time you will reclaim your breath and retrain yourself to breathe properly.

NOTES

"proper" breathing put my mind
at ease almost falling asleep.
I then purposely thought of a
stressful situation to watch the
change in my breathing and
noticed shorter breaths and even my
heart racing went back to slower
deeper breaths and instantly felt
calm again.

NOTES

NOTES

NOTES

NOTES

Chapter Three

Synchronicity: Noticing Life's Hidden Messages

L ife is easy for most of us to understand in reverse. How many times have you thought about an event in your life that happened to you days, months, or even years after it occurred and had an "ah-ha" moment? You truly came to understand that the event was a lesson and it taught you something incredibly important.

What if I told you that this kind of thing is occurring in your life every day, in every moment, but most of us are too distracted to realize? It's true. A majority of our life lessons slip by unnoticed. It doesn't have to be this way.

Have you heard of synchronicity? It's a concept popularized in modern times by Carl Jung. Jung's theory was that our lives are a series of events, seemingly unrelated, that are what he coined as, "meaningful coincidences." It's these meaningful coincidences that we begin to notice once our minds are uncluttered and our souls begin to settle into their natural state of rest.

When I find myself feeling lost or perplexed about something that happens in my life I've learned to always ask, "Why is this happening?" or "What is try-ing to happen here?" I've learned through my many years of meditation practice that this physical world is just like our schoolhouse and the events in life are our greatest teachers. The universe we live in is an interactive web that is trying to teach us lessons continuously in real time. Often, the lessons are small and harmless. Sometimes, especially if we don't learn them the first few attempts, they can become more harsh and life altering.

I've learned to view life as a theater production that is being performed for each specific person to learn from. I think William Shakespeare realized this when he wrote, *"All the world's a stage, And all the men and women merely players; They have their exits and their entrances, And one man in his time plays many parts, His acts being seven ages…"*

Meditation sparks substantial shifts in your perception that open you up to subtler aspects of life. This process can greatly improve and deepen the quality of your time on this Earth. Once you begin to notice synchronicity and understand how it works, it will show you that our reality isn't some series of random events but rather meaningful coincidences. After a while, you will come to understand that there's either a lesson to learn or a lesson to teach others in nearly every moment.

One of the great secrets of life is that our three-dimensional reality is providing us with guidance and support in real time, in every single moment. When you feel this and come to know it's true, it provides immeasurable freedom and comfort.

Opening your heart and mind to the beautiful concept of synchronicity will change your life quickly. You will find your luck will seem to get better, you will enjoy more and suffer less, and will be "in the right place at the right time" much more often. Life will feel easier and less stressful. Why is this? You will begin to understand the "why" of events that before seemed totally random and without meaning. You will no longer be swimming against the current of life but you will be traveling right along with it and it will propel you towards your destiny.

One pitfall I caution you to avoid is overthinking. There is no need to overanalyze every moment of your life to understand how synchronicity works. Simply start being present, staying centered in the current moment, and paying attention to the life events unfolding before you. Overthinking will leave you lost in a mental maze, like a hall of mirrors that will make meaningful coincidences even more difficult to recognize.

⚹ Pay extra attention to moments that feel special or important to you, even if you can't explain why. I'm talking about the moments in your life that give you goosebumps or make the hairs on the back of your neck stand up. Have you ever had a thought or an idea some upon you spontaneously that you simply can't get out of your head? How about a moment where you suddenly feel extreme joy, comfort, or despair for no apparent particular reason? These moments are typically where the important lessons are to be found. Learn to listen to and trust your intuition during these times. Most importantly, don't ignore them. ⸼

You don't need an authority figure or a spiritual intermediary to begin using synchronicity as a tool for your own personal development. You already possess all of the power you'll ever need within you. The only thing required of you is to believe in the concept of meaningful occurrences and to be present in the moment and pay attention. Soon your powers of observation and deciphering will start to evolve. Meditation allows you to master this quickly.

⸼ Lessons can even be found in our dreams. They come through imagery and symbolism, but we must use our intuition to decipher their true meaning. For this reason, I recommend keeping a notebook near your bed to write down any dreams you remember when you first wake up. If you don't do this, the details of the dream quickly fade away.

We've all had moments where a song pops into our heads and then we hear it on the radio or television shortly after. Sometimes we'll be thinking of a friend and they'll call us a few minutes later. There are times you'll be watching a film or documentary and will feel as though it gives you the exact answers you have been seeking. These are all examples of how synchronicity works to give us a preview of what will happen or provide a nudge in the right direction.

Once you become a true student and recognize the guidance and support the universe provides, you will learn your life lessons much more quickly. Your evolution will begin to grow at a faster pace than you ever imagined. Why? Because your life will truly be, "in sync" with the universe.

After a while you will notice synchronicity all the time. You will begin to co-create your own reality and the quality of your own life through your own intentions and expectations. If you expect to have a positive life experience, this is exactly the kind of life you will start to attract. One thing you will learn quickly is if you expect that people will be accepting and loving, the chances are greater that they will be. It may sound overly simplistic, but after you meditate for a while you will find it to be true.

The comfort and power that you feel when you become a student of life is indescribable. The beautiful language of synchronicity will change your life in ways you can't currently comprehend.

One thing you will start to notice as you begin to live a meditation-centered life is how certain aspects of the physical world you once thought were static start to seem more fluid. There will be a plasticity to things that you once thought were fixed units of measure. They can be shaped by our consciousness. Consider the old quote, "A watched pot never boils." is so true. When we control our world, our perception of time can be sped up and slowed down at will. Our perception of time is slowed down the moment we put our attention on it. When you are bored or something is stressful or unenjoyable to you, you pay more attention to time and time seems to pass at a snail's pace. On the flip-side, when you are doing something that is fun, an activity you thoroughly enjoy, you pay less attention to the time passing and therefore time seems to pass more quickly.

PUTTING IT INTO PRACTICE

Synchronicity

For the next week pay attention to moments in your life that have a special feeling, gravity, or merely capture your attention for unexplainable reasons. These moments don't have to be earth-shattering occurrences, most often these are minor things.

Record the moments of synchronicity you notice throughout the day in this chapter's *Notes* section, revisit this often and then think about what meaning or lesson might lay in them for you. After you get into the practice of noticing these moments you will notice them more and more.

Time

Let's do a simple experiment related to the old, "A watched pot never boils" quote. This will demonstrate the plasticity of our perception of time. Grab a tea kettle, or a large pan, fill it with water and heat it up on the stove on the highest setting. Stand right in front of it and watch it until it boils. It probably seems like it took forever.

Now, drain out the hot water and fill it up with fresh, cool water. Put it on the burner and heat it up in the same way as you did before, except don't place your attention on the stove. Browse the internet on your phone or read a book. The water seemed to boil much faster the second time, didn't it?

Learn to use this variance in perception to improve the quality of your life. The next time you are waiting for a bus or a train, you're on a long flight, or doing something that makes time feel like it is passing too slowly, relax, take some deep breaths and do whatever you can to take your attention off of the fact that you're waiting. Read a book, play a game, or listen to a podcast.

Use the time that you would normally waste being agitated or restless to learn something. By focusing your attention on something other than passing time, it will make the minutes seem to go by more quickly.

If you are on vacation, visiting with friends, or even enjoying the weekend and you want time to pass more slowly, simply learn to be present. Don't let worry or your imagination take you away from the moment, be cognizant of the passing minutes. If you do this time will appear to slow down.

Start experimenting with your perception of passing time and witness what a real difference it can make. Use the *Notes* section at the end of this chapter to document your results.

NOTES

- Spending time with the family rather than spending a night out w/ the girls at the club!
    - lessons?? No drinking, more fun w/ the family—realizing family is more important while a night out would have been something temporary or not even a good time @ all, instead time wasted <u>OR</u> a night of regret and remorse. realizing being w/ my family makes me <u>truly</u> happy!

- Going to court and coming out on conditional releace (would much rather take that than <u>any more</u> jail time!)

- Having someone like Alm in my life, although the relationship is a bit odd I do appreciate all his help and input, its put a huge impact on my stress for everything recent thats been goin on.

NOTES

NOTES

NOTES

NOTES

Chapter Four

Conquering Fear
Do One Thing A Day That Scares You

What is the key to conquering your worst fear? All you need to do is one small thing per day that scares you.

Believe me, I know. I suffered from debilitating depression in my early twenties. Why? I got into a practice of not facing my fears. Instead, I ran away from them. Each time I did this I became more disappointed in myself and as a result the fear gained power and my self-confidence decreased a little each time. The accumulative value of these little (and sometimes big) disappointments in myself over the years contributed greatly to the anxiety and depression that eventually gained complete control of my life.

I would guess that this is a common cause of depression and anxiety for a lot of people. Throughout my years of meditation, I've learned a few things about facing fear. The most important thing I've discovered is that fear itself is both a bully and a coward. If you start standing up to your fears, even if you do it a little at a time, your confidence will grow. The fears will begin to have less and less power over you.

Very few of us were born brave but this doesn't mean bravery can't be mastered. When I was young, I was terrified of public speaking. I mean terrified. Countless opportunities were passed up because of this fear. I'm ashamed to admit that one of the reasons I didn't finish college was I was trying to avoid the anxiety of group discussions and speeches. I even passed up the chance to give a best man speech at my brother's first wedding because of this fear.

Everything began to change when I started to challenge this horrible bully that was so severely limiting my life. I started small. First I made it a point to speak up in morning meetings at work. Each time I did, I gained more confidence and felt a tiny rush of inner pride.

After a few years of challenging myself to take more risks, I agreed to co-facilitate a meditation class at work. There were about fifty people in the audience and it was a huge success. That same year I gave a best man speech at my brother's second wedding. To my surprise, the wedding planner approached me afterwards and complimented me on that speech!

My point is, I kept picking away at this fear with every opportunity that presented itself, and this is the key to conquering any fear. I kept raising my level of tolerance and confidence until fear no longer had a hold on me. Since then, I've appeared on radio and television to promote my books, been interviewed on a podcast, given speeches in front of hundreds of people, and now teach weekly meditation classes. Any fear can be conquered.

It's helpful to spend time with people who already have the attributes that you wish to gain. I'm naturally an introvert and one of my good friends is extremely outgoing. We go to Chicago every year for a long weekend of food, music, and sightseeing. He can easily strike up conversations with people he's never met. As a result no one seems like a stranger; we've gotten some of the best advice, and have met some incredibly interesting people. By the end of the weekend I find that I'm much more outgoing just from spending time with him.

PUTTING IT INTO PRACTICE

Think about one fear you have, large or small, that you would like to get rid of. Contemplate how this fear limits your life and how that limitation makes you feel. Now, make a solemn commitment to take a small step each day towards conquering it.

Start very small if you need to, but the important thing is to start.

For example, if you're naturally shy around new people make it a point to make eye contact and say hello to a stranger in an elevator. Then the next day strike up a simple conversation. Again, taking incremental but systematic steps in challenging your fears are the key to success.

If heights are your fear, the next time you're in a tall building walk up to the window, take a deep breath, and force yourself to look out at the landscape and then down to the street. Whatever your fears are all it takes are small measures each day to desensitize yourself from them. With dedication and effort eventually you'll conquer them.

Write down one fear you would like to work on this week. Each day take a small step to challenge that fear. Document your results at the end of every day. Once you feel as though you've beaten that bully, choose your next target, another of your fears and repeat the same steps. After a while, your list of fears will be considerably shorter or possibly even non-existent. Once you experience the confidence gained from this practice, it become a mission to slay all of your fears one by one.

Do you want to be more successful, happier, and have a greater sense of self-confidence? If so, do one small thing every day that scares you.

Success

Both a seeker
and a scarred sage
I am approaching
that certain age
when you
learn that
each decision
matters.

Fear is both
a bully and
a coward
stand up to it
more than
once and it
shatters

Mine heart
has felt
the glory
of the dawning
of this dream
to be found
a few steps
beyond the
searing pain
of defeat

Each time
you fall
you must rise
again
to your feet
because with
persistence
you will win
and this
success is
so sweet.

~ ERIC VANCE WALTON

NOTES

Fears — shy, timid around new ppl new things
- Driving around new/unfamiliar places
- Being in a totally new atmosphere
  - going to school (Because its diff)
  - OR career change / new Jobs
- Speaking in front of a group of ppl

NOTES

NOTES

NOTES

NOTES

NOTES

Chapter Five

Perception/Focus on the Positive

"There are only two ways to live your life. One is as though nothing is a miracle. The other is as though everything is a miracle."

~ ALBERT EINSTEIN

Have you ever had a day or even a few hours where everything felt as though it flowed perfectly and the things you do seem effortless? This feels spectacular, doesn't it? During days like this, your productivity is amazing and your energy level seems almost infinite. Even if challenges arise, we can stay level-headed and find a quick solution to whatever problem is trying to plague us. When we are in this positive frame of mind we feel a sense of hope, our mood is upbeat, and the world seems like a beautiful place.

On the other side of the spectrum, we've all had those days where we've felt clumsy, out of sync with everyone and everything around us, and like nothing is going our way. Despite our best efforts, we can't get anything done, can't focus, and feel tired and depleted. We are moody, suspicious of other people's intentions, and the world seems like a dark and dangerous place.

What is the difference between these two kinds of days? It all comes down to your frame of mind and how your mood filters the events that are unfolding in your life in real time.

What if I told you that—today and every day—you have huge degree of control over which of those two kinds of experiences you have? Do you most often choose positive or negative? The truth is, you do have considerable control. You can choose to be miserable or you can choose to be happy. You are not a victim of circumstance, the quality of your life is determined to a large degree by your perception of it.

Allow me to explain. In our physical universe, like attracts like. If you walk around with a general feeling of dread and hopelessness, you will attract a flood of negativity into your life. If your mood is upbeat and positive, these are the life experience you will attract. Again, like attracts like.

As you begin to regularly meditate you will naturally become more positive as you increase your mindfulness and by doing so you will attract an abundance of positive experiences into your life. Don't take my word for it: once you begin your regular meditation practice and you will see for yourself.

Change

Imagine a terrible thunderstorm with driving rain, lightning and terrible winds. It is the trees that are flexible and bend in the wind that have the best chances of survival. The trees that stand rigid are usually damaged or destroyed. The same holds true for life. We must learn to keep a somewhat open mind and not always fight change. Change is scary for almost everyone but it is sometimes necessary to better our circumstances.

In this life, change is the only constant. Change, on some level, happens all around us in every moment of every day. In this rapidly evolving world, those who are the most successful in life are those who manage change well. Our ability to deal positively with change greatly affects the quality of our lives.

Happiness

"Happiness doesn't come from having the best
of everything but making the best of everything."

~ GAIL LYNNE GOODWIN

Happiness and fulfillment are our soul's guidepost. During your meditation practice, as in life, your level of happiness and fulfillment are our indicators that tell us if we're moving forward or slipping backwards. If you are unhappy, your soul is merely trying to tell you that there is something in your internal or external environment that isn't right and needs to change. Fortunately, you are the person who is best suited for the job of creating this positive change in your life.

So if you find yourself in a funk ask yourself, "Why am I feeling this way?"

A regular routine of meditation gives you the tools necessary to make clear-headed decisions and deal positively with change. Not unlike a lot of things in life, if you keep up your practice you will see real, tangible results. Keep in mind that meditation isn't always easy, but is a very honest practice. You receive out of it exactly what you put into it. Don't expect miracles right away but one thing is for sure; with continued and dedicated practice, tangible gifts will begin to materialize in your life.

Regain Control

"Man is free at the moment he wishes to be."

~ VOLTAIRE

How many of us have found ourselves in situations that feel like they're careening out of control? Our thoughts can easily send us into a downward spiral of negative emotions like rage, jealousy, or fear. In this physical world, we don't always have control over the things that happen to us but we can have control over how our brain processes the events and our reactions to these external influences. Most of us have been conditioned to react subconsciously to certain situations that arise in our environment. We don't take the time to think or to analyze.

These automatic emotional reactions can easily spin out of control and result in embarrassment or damaged relationships. How would you like to not only take steps to better your external circumstances but also have the freedom to react to those inevitable, unpleasant external conditions with clear headed confidence and poise? Among the countless benefits of regular meditation is the freedom from those seemingly uncontrollable emotional reactions of anger, jealousy and fear that we usually end up regretting.

A common trait of those who regularly meditate is their ability to control the most important instrument in the world, their own minds. Just as a virtuoso perfects the playing of an instrument, a person who meditates learns to be the master of his or her own mind. What could you accomplish in this world if you controlled your thoughts instead of your thoughts controlling you?

NOTES

— Anything, really...
   — Accomplishing school goals
   — career changee
   — over coming the fear of being in
a new at mosphere
   — talking to new ppl or even being
around them
   — being able to spark up a converSation
first.

NOTES

NOTES

NOTES

NOTES

48

NOTES

Chapter Six

Gratitude
The Best State to Reside In

It can be so easy to get swept up into a stream of anxiety and worry. As a writer, there's always that next book or that next article deadline. At this point in my career, it can sometimes feel nearly impossible to find enough time for everyone and everything in life. What I've discovered is most of this anxiety and worry is completely imagined, caused by faulty perception. It's amazing how quickly these feelings of anxiety and worry can be shut down instantly through a very simple shift in mindset.

"Happiness cannot be traveled to, owned, earned, worn or consumed. Happiness is the spiritual experience of living every minute with love, grace, and gratitude."

~ Denis Waitley

Sometimes this state of gratitude happens spontaneously. For example, I was feeling stressed about preparing two books for publication this year and keeping up with my social media and freelance work. There I was, was walking our beagle in the biting, subzero January wind of Minnesota and cursing it. My face was scrunched up, my shoulders tense. Suddenly, an overwhelming warmth washed over me. The only way I can accurately describe it was a general feeling of content. That feeling was, "I am so thankful for my life. I am perfectly happy in this very moment."

Instantly, the stress and worry melted away and I relaxed. Even the frigid wind didn't seem so bad. After meditating for nearly a quarter century I realize how vital it is to keep our consciousness in this state of gratitude for as long and as often as we possibly can.

Why is residing in a state of gratitude so important?

First of all, striving to live in a state of gratitude makes us happier. This should be reason enough. Even more importantly, though, when we're living in this state, we open the floodgates for more positive experiences and abundance to flow into our lives. This is how the subtle energies of our universe work. Like attracts like. You attract to you whatever thoughts and emotions continuously loop in your mind. This doesn't mean passive acceptance of the bad things in your life but acknowledgement of the good. I repeat, living in gratitude doesn't mean passive acceptance of all things. If you don't believe that working to dwell in a state of gratitude for the wonderful things in your life works, I urge you to try it for a week.

There are a few, very simple, exercises called Mantra to help us to quickly ease into this state of gratitude. A Mantra is a sacred practice of repeating certain words or groups of words. These words are sacred to many Hindus and Buddhists and the repetition of them are believed to bring about great blessings and states of enlightenment to the person uttering them either aloud or silently.

Many English speakers who practice the art of mantra repeat the traditional Sanskrit phrases. I don't do this because I believe having to think about the meaning of the words hinders the intended process. In my personal practice I repeat the English translations of classic Sanskrit mantra. For example, in Sanskrit the mantra, Dhanya Vad translated into English is, "I feel gratitude" and Kritajna

Hum means, "I am gratitude." These two mantra have worked very well for me. *"Give yourself a gift of five minutes of contemplation in awe of everything you see around you. Go outside and turn your attention to the many miracles around you. This five-minute-a-day regimen of appreciation and gratitude will help you to focus your life in awe."*

~Wayne Dyer

Whenever you feel negative, depressed, or sad I urge you to try the following exercise:

Inhale for a count of 5;
Hold your breath for a count of 5; and
Exhale for a count of 5.

Repeat the following mantra until you feel your negative state of mind slip away:

I am gratitude.
I am gratitude.
I am gratitude.

I feel gratitude.
I feel gratitude.
I feel gratitude.

Another, even easier to remember, mantra is "I'm thankful for...." and you can go on a recite anything that you can think of that you're thankful for in your life. Objects of gratitude be clean air, good health, fresh water, ample food, a pet, a job, a car, a friend or significant other...literally anything.

These mantra are simple enough to easily remember but are very powerful and can be practiced silently anywhere. I particularly like to practice them while walking. There's something about the rhythmic sound of footsteps that make the recitation of mantra especially effective.

NOTES

NOTES

NOTES

NOTES

NOTES

Chapter Seven

Step Away From the Negatives
(and no one will get hurt)

As you get deeper into your meditation practice you will find you have increased tolerance for most things, but one thing you will have less tolerance for is chronic negativity. There are many negative things in life that are unavoidable but your exposure to those things and people that have a negative impact on your well being can be reduced or totally avoided. Think of your personal happiness as a savings account. Exposing yourself to negativity of any kind and allowing it to influence you is a withdrawal from your Happiness Account. Optimism, enthusiasm, and positive behavior that builds your confidence is a deposit into the Happiness Account. Each day you must ask yourself, *"What is the balance of my Happiness Account?"*

One of my mentors, James Altucher says, "We are the sum of the five people we spend the most time with." A good rule of thumb when you begin to live a meditation-centered life is to pay attention to those who make you feel good or make you feel bad. You will find that feeling good and staying positive is addictive. It took me well over three decades to realize the extent to which the company I kept affected my life. Once we become conscious of this we can make better decisions about who we share our lives with.

Some people are simply addicted to gossip, misery, complaining, and drama. These are toxic people. We can still love them but it's best to love them from afar.

The old saying, "Misery loves company" is an absolute truth. Being subjected to this toxic behavior can affect you in a negative way even if you don't realize it.

It's admirable for us to be empathetic. But it's equally as important to become cognizant of chronic complainers. These are people who always find themselves immersed in negativity and are locked into a pattern of this kind of behavior. These are people who aren't learning their life lessons and often need professional help.

One reason toxic people don't learn their life lessons is because they seek out and surround themselves with people who tolerate and enable their negative behavior. Reclaim your life, give yourself permission to spend less time with these people and your life will noticeably improve.

Be conscious about who you spend your time with. Learn to primarily surround yourself with positive people who make you feel good. People who are supportive, genuinely happy with your success, and don't resent you for it. Make it a habit to spend your time with those who are actively working to improve their own lives. If you make these changes, the balance of your Happiness Account will grow exponentially. I also make it a practice to also include a few mentors in my circle of friends who are smarter, more successful, and have the qualities and traits I wish to acquire.

Another very important thing is to constantly be aware of the quality of our own thoughts. Dwelling in the past, limiting beliefs, complaining, worrying about the future, negative self-talk, the need to be right all of the time, blaming others, seeking approval from others, fearing or resisting change, the need to impress others, these are all attributes that inhibit your growth towards true and lasting happiness. They prevent you from becoming your best self.

Remember, like it or not, you are slowing absorbing the traits of those you spend your time with. Consciously ask yourself, *"Do I want to become like them?"* If the answer is no, consider being around them less and try incorporating new people into your life who have traits you would like to have yourself.

PUTTING IT INTO PRACTICE

Using the *Notes* section at the end of this chapter list five things (these can be habits, situations, or people) that make you feel unhappy, less confident, or sad.

Dwell on this list and think about the ripple effect this has and how many other aspects of your life these things have a negative affect on. Imagine how your life might improve if you spend less time or give less attention to these things. Now, work each day on making your life more positive by eliminating as much unnecessary drama and negativity as you can from your life.

NOTES

- A1on, -- Being / hanging out with him may or is temporary happiness and often times they in that moment. Afterwards I am left feeling empty, sad, unhappy and disappointed -- most times I really wont hear from him just neeeuy whenever it is convenient to him or the next time we are hanging out, which also is usually typically on his time.

- Going out @ night — the ripple effects have caused me to get more than one DUI not oney that but im losing time w/ son and family which leaves me feeling guilty. DUI case - kinda goes hand in hand with the bullet listed above this but has caused me more stress than ever, I constantly think about the consequences which scare me but the cost of the but has made a huge impact on how I can spend my money and will have to budget wisely.

NOTES

— my life situation right now — often think
about where I am in life and how much
further I wish I was career, living /
and relationship wise.

NOTES

NOTES

NOTES

Chapter Eight

Making Yourself A Clear Channel

—

We've all experienced the frustration of a slow Wi-fi or cellular connection. It can take forever to download what you're trying to access. It's the same way with the human mind. Regular meditation will heal us no matter what but if our minds are cloudy and our bodies aren't as healthy as they can be, it will take longer. If you want to feel the optimum benefits connecting ourselves to that source of deep wisdom and knowledge in our universe through meditation we must first make ourselves a clear channel. To do this you must have proper sleep, nutrition, and fitness levels.

Sleep

Sleep is the best performance enhancer in the world. Without the proper amount of sleep, our bodies and minds can't operate at peak efficiency and everything suffers, including our health and productivity. If we're not operating at peak efficiency our enjoyment of life is diminished and it's more difficult to be in the present moment.

Geneticists have discovered that a small percentage of the population has a gene mutation. These people have a, "short sleeper" gene that allows them to function perfectly on four to five hours of sleep. These are extremely lucky people and I wish I was one of them but I'm not. The rest of us need somewhere between seven and nine hours per night, the equivalent of one third of your day, of quality sleep to be our most productive and healthy.

Start paying attention to how you feel when you wake up in the morning. How many hours of sleep does it take you to feel your best? For most people the ideal number is seven to eight hours of sleep. It's important that you find your ideal number and make it a goal to get this amount every night. Then you must integrate a sleep ritual into your life that assures you stay healthy and operate at peak efficiency.

Sustenance — You Are What You Eat

"Gluttony is an emotional escape, a sign that something is eating us."

~ Peter De Vries

Obesity is at epidemic proportions and is now the second leading premature cause of death behind heart disease. We all know someone who's taken a ride on the rollercoaster. They seem to jump from one fad diet to another and become obsessed with their weight. Modern science has proven that losing and gaining vast amounts of weight over a lifetime can be even more dangerous than being a little overweight. Believe it or not, your diet affects more than just your waistline. A healthier diet is good for the mind as well as the body. Simply put, what we put into our bodies is what we become. Literally and definitely figuratively!

Listen to the cues your body is giving you. At some time we've all experienced that heavy, bloated feeling of indigestion. This is our body telling us that we're either overindulging or we're feeding it the wrong foods. Not everyone is ready to become strict vegetarians, though, you don't have to be. A simple rule regarding food is the less processed the better.

Educate yourself about the food you eat. Learn where your food comes and how it's processed. Try to buy locally sourced food and eat organic. The same holds true if you eat meat, the less processed the better. Free range, grass-fed, antibiotic/hormone/preservative free meat is best. Steer clear or reduce your intake of hydrogenated oils or trans fats, saturated fats, artificial sweeteners of any kind, and processed or convenience foods. Find out more about alternative sweeteners such as stevia, honey, or xylitol. Also, explore the benefits of drinking black, green, or white tea.

I've found nothing to be as invigorating and detoxifying in the morning as drinking warm lemon water. This is such a simple thing to integrate into your daily routine. Warm lemon water, mixed with fresh juice of organic lemons, wakes you up and keeps you alert without caffeine. It also has a healthy dose of vitamin C and, despite the lemon's acidity, it actually makes your body more alkaline. Research shows that if your body is alkaline you will be far less susceptible to illness and disease.

Here's a simple recipe for lemon water:
- 2 Tbsp fresh squeezed (or cold-pressed bottled) organic lemon juice;
- 8-12 oz of lukewarm (not hot) water.

The best time to drink warm lemon water immediately after waking in the morning, on an empty stomach, and wait thirty minutes before eating anything. Also, use a straw so the acid in the lemon doesn't affect your tooth enamel. It's that simple. I drink it just as described above but you can sweeten with a little local, organic honey or even add a dash of cayenne pepper powder for further detoxifying benefits.

Another great addition to any diet are fermented foods like yogurt, kefir, sauerkraut, kimchi (spicy Korean sauerkraut) and kombucha (fermented tea). Most ancient cultures had this figured out but it's something we've lost. New research suggests the health of your gut and your mental health are more intertwined than previously thought. Fermented foods are rich in probiotics which replenish healthy microbes in your digestive tract. Probiotics improve your immune system, digestion, and possibly even your mental health. I drink grass fed kefir daily, kombucha occasionally (GT's is my favorite brand - http://synergydrinks.com), and also keep a jar of organic sauerkraut around and have a little as a side dish with dinner every few days.

A healthy diet might seem like it's a little more expensive but in the long term, it will greatly add to the quality your life and save you money in the form of fewer unplanned days off work and reduced healthcare costs, plus you'll feel better. You'll also have more energy and a clearer head. To reduce food costs, check into becoming a member of a food co-op in your area or buy from local farms or farmers markets.

If more people followed these simple steps, they wouldn't have to subject themselves to the psychological and physical stresses of the dietary roller coaster. Also, those who perpetuate and get rich off of this unhealthy mindset of gorging ourselves and "purging" would be out of business.

Physical Activity

Our bodies were made to move and the key to our physical well-being is to make sure we do just that. The easiest way to ensure you get the exercise you need every day is to integrate as much movement into your daily routine as you can. Park as far away as possible from your workplace or bike to work if you can. I park about a mile away from the building I work in, so this is a guaranteed two miles of walking per day. I also bike to work when the weather permits.

The key to sticking with an exercise regime is it must be fun. You have to enjoy the exercises enough so that they don't seem like a chore to you. Low impact exercises like walking, cycling, dancing, roller skating, swimming, yoga, or tai chi can be done by people of most fitness levels and ages. What activities did you really enjoy as a child? If they made you happy then, chances are they will now. My favorite activity as a child was always riding my bike. I still love cycling almost forty years later. Rediscover activities that once interested you as a child and they will pay the dividends of greater enjoyment and health to your life.

The truth is not everyone has the genetics required to resemble society's idea of what a model should look like. But you know what? Not all people who look like models are healthy. Healthy bodies come in all shapes and sizes. The most important thing is that you move every day, feel good, and are happy with how you look and feel. Nothing else matters.

PUTTING IT INTO PRACTICE

Over the next seven days, make a conscious effort to pay attention to your sleep, diet, and actively level.

SLEEP. Using the Notes feature of this chapter track the number of hours you sleep for the next seven days and briefly document how you felt throughout each day. The one or two waking hours you will "lose" by allowing yourself proper sleep will more than made up for in increased productivity. Remember, busyness doesn't not always equal productivity.

SUSTENANCE. Pay attention to the kinds of foods you eat for the next week. Don't rush during meal time. Focus on the flavors and textures of what you're eating and chew your food carefully. Make an effort to eat less refined foods (including sugar) and eat more organic fruits, vegetables, nuts, and healthy lean meats and fish. Also, make a conscious effort to listen to your body. If you are hungry, eat. If you aren't that hungry, even if it's meal time, eat less. Pick one of the fermented foods mentioned in this chapter and make it a part of your daily diet. Using the Notes section, document how you feel once you begin to eat this way.

PHYSICAL ACTIVITY. Integrate movement into your daily routine. Set a fitness goal for the next week. This doesn't have to be extreme but try to at least walk a little every day. Remember, walks are a great opportunity to practice your deep, conscious breathing. At least three times per week, try something a little more vigorous like a bike ride, stream a free yoga session on YouTube, or strap on your headphones and dance for fifteen or twenty minutes. Note how much different you feel physically and mentally afterwards. You tend to feel the benefits from exercise almost immediately.

NOTES

Sleep

Sustenance

Physical Activity

NOTES

Sleep

Sustenance

Physical Activity

NOTES

Sleep

Sustenance

Physical Activity

NOTES

Sleep

Sustenance

Physical Activity

NOTES

Sleep

Sustenance

Physical Activity

Chapter Nine

Simplify

"A man is rich in proportion to the number of things he can let alone."

~ HENRY DAVID THOREAU

Thoreau was a wise one, indeed. To find true peace in our lives, we must continually strive to keep our consciousness more in the present moment. The problem is that the modern world in which we live provides countless distractions that prevent us from staying anchored in the present moment. As a result, most of us feel overworked and stressed. We feel desperate for some kind of peace and stability.

We have been conditioned to believe that abundance is wealth, busyness and multitasking equals productivity, and that we feel overworked even though the true cause is our own inefficiency. In our modern world, quantity has replaced quality in almost every conceivable way. Meditation will help you to simplify your life, become more aware of imbalances, re-shift your priorities, and greatly increase your quality of life.

Technology

Do you ever feel like there aren't enough hours in the day? I know I do. We live in a time of frenetic technological advancement. Computers double their abilities every twelve to eighteen months. It seems that technology is evolving faster than our ability to adapt to it. We must find a way to better balance our lives because the technology in our world is evolving exponentially.

There was a time, not long ago, when cell phones only did two things: made and received calls. Now, they give us instant access to everything, including social media. Social media taps into one of our greatest human desires to socialize. By way of our mobile phones, we can connect with thousands of people simultaneously, whenever we choose. We can now feel the same joy and sense of interconnectedness we used to experience from face-to-face interaction at any time by logging into our social media accounts.

Mobile phones are your single greatest tool, if used with discipline. Sadly, cellphones have also become society's number one addiction and largest impediment to keeping our consciousness in the present moment. Mobile phone addiction is an epidemic but its negative effects are only starting to be recognized. The warning signs are everywhere: zoned out children; distracted walking; people staring at their screens while completely ignoring friends and family with whom they could be having enriching conversations.

Using technology to your benefit instead of your detriment merely takes discipline and restraint. How many hours per day do you spend on your smart phone? If you're anything like me, when you begin to pay attention, the number will surprise you.

The key to regaining life balance is screen-time management. When you're socializing, make a conscious effort to be present and engaged with those around you. Put your phone away and vow to not to look at it. Suggest that those you're with to do the same. I remember a time when even glancing at your wristwatch while socializing was considered rude because it implied disinterest. Time is, by far, our most precious commodity. The people you're sharing your time with deserve your full attention just as much as you deserve theirs.

When you're staring at your phone, you could be also missing synchronistic moments that hold life-changing potential. For this reason, try to set strict screen-time limits for yourself throughout the day. Try limiting yourself to an hour in the morning and an hour in the afternoon. There are multiple free apps available for both Android and iPhone to assist with this if you find it too difficult a task to accomplish on your own. Search, "screen-time management" in Google Play or iTunes.

Reclaiming your power and freedom from technology will be one of the single best decisions you can make to improve the quality of your life. Like every aspect of life, balance and discipline are the keys. Use technology, don't let it use you.

Focus

I place the blame for the concept of multitasking squarely on the Industrial Revolution. Before this time, people tended to focus on one task at a time. Today, multitasking is held in such high regard that it's one of the top keywords used on resumes and job descriptions throughout the world, right up there with "self-starter." A certain amount of multitasking is necessary to function in our world, but when you try to accomplish too much at once, everything we are trying to accomplish suffers.

One horrible side effect of multitasking is the inability to concentrate. The good news is, with continued practice, meditation will help to redevelop and strengthen your ability to concentrate. This is one of the many areas in which mediation will assist you that doesn't require any conscious effort. All that is required is you diligently continue your daily meditation practice.

Your "Stuff"

I believe that the condition of your living space both directly influences your mood and state of well-being and is outward physical representation of the state of your mind. Take a look around at your living space. Is it clean and orderly or messy and cluttered? It's so much easier to relax when your space is clean and everything is in its place. You will find as your meditation progresses you will naturally prefer to have a tidy living space.

Marie Kondo wrote a very enlightening book on this topic called, "The

Life-Changing Magic of Tidying Up: The Japanese Art of Decluttering and Organizing." Her book made me completely rethink my relationship to my possessions and my living space. After I read her book, I immediately began to declutter my entire life. I gave away or sold possessions that I had accumulated over the years that I didn't use or no longer brought me joy.

For decades, marketing firms have been paid millions (probably more like billions) of dollars to condition us all to focus on initial price instead of lifetime cost of ownership. This makes companies much more money. It's worked. To quickly get de-conditioned to this trick you merely have to start thinking about true cost of ownership for both the goods and services in your life.

For example, my wife and I started thinking about the annual cost of satellite television. Once we calculated how much of our income was going out annually for cable/satellite T.V., we cancelled our subscription immediately. Instead, we bought a digital antenna for $20 and a refurbished Apple TV for $70. For years we've survived happily with this set-up. We find we watch less television and have reduced our overall television bill from $130 per month to $20. Whenever you can reduce your budget like this it equates to an instant increase in salary.

I've also learned to buy things that will last and can be repaired instead of buying disposable items that can just be used for a short amount of time and thrown away. For example, I was spending $20 a month on modern, disposable razor blades. This really bothered me. I did some research and purchased a razor that uses old-fashioned safety blades. The razor was twenty dollars and is made in Germany (Merkur brand) and is of super high quality. I found two hundred safety blades online for twenty dollars. Five years later I'm still using that same box of blades and I'm actually getting a better shave. I've also saved over a thousand dollars in the process.

My greatest bargain was a 1959 English-made Raleigh 3-speed bicycle I found on Craiglist for the price of a department store bike. Each and every part of the vintage bike is made so it can be repaired, even the pedals. The Raleigh bike is now my main rider, the craftsmanship is so much better than modern bikes that I eventually sold all of my other ones because they couldn't compare in terms of quality.

Learning to be satisfied with less reduces your overall stress and magnifies your overall happiness. This state of satisfaction begins with being grateful for what you have right now. Make it a practice, either before or after your meditation sessions, to think about all of the blessings in your life. Once you start focusing on gratitude for what you have, the hunger to acquire things you don't have will lessen.

You will find there's an amazing freedom from not feeling tethered an overabundance of possessions. Through meditation, as you begin to get glimpses of true happiness, you'll realize that material things can in no way compare to the real thing.

Reboot Your Consciousness

When modern life leaves you feeling frazzled and exhausted, the best antidote is a simple walk in the woods. Humans have evolved over hundreds of thousands of years with regular contact with nature. Only recently have humans begun to spend most of their time indoors. Our genes simply haven't had time to catch up to this major shift in behavior.

A walk in the woods is like rebooting our human consciousness. Nature allows us to clear our minds and find our natural balance again. Research even shows listening to birdsong can improve mood and cognitive function. When I'm feeling stressed, or if I'm experiencing writer's block, a walk in the woods never fails to help.

PUTTING IT INTO PRACTICE

Use the *Notes* feature of this chapter to document the changes you notice as a result of these practices.

TECHNOLOGY. Evaluate how much time you spend on your mobile phone daily. Then, ask yourself, "Could I be making better use of that time?" If the answer is yes, set an alarm on your phone to chime twice daily. Use this block of 15-30 minutes twice daily as your allotted social media screen time.

Also, when you're socializing with others, keep your phone in your pocket or purse. Encourage your friends and family to do the same.

FOCUS. As you continue your meditation practice take notice of any changes in your ability to focus. As you're living your day-to-day life start paying attention to your behavior throughout the day. You will find that you're more likely to feel stressed when you're multitasking. Sometimes multitasking is unavoidable but most times it is not, you've just been conditioned to believe that you're being more efficient by doing it. Practice concentrating on one thing at a time. If you're walking…just walk, if you're cooking…just cook, if you're sweeping the floor…just sweep. At first your brain will scream, "You could be doing more!" but keep up your focus on the singular task until it is done. Try this once a day and then record in the Notes section of this chapter how it makes you feel.

YOUR STUFF. Take one hour and evaluate your living space. Begin to shed unneeded or unwanted possessions. Is there anything you own that you'd like to donate to charity? Do you have anything you'd like to sell to make a little extra money for a dream trip or activity you've always wanted to do? Is there anything that you no longer use that might be of use to someone else?

Your clothes closet is a great place to start. I have a practice of donating any item of clothing that I haven't worn for six months or more to charity. One helpful way to evaluate which clothes are getting wear-time is to turn all of the hangers so your clothes are facing backwards. When an item is worn and rehung, turn that hanger so it's facing forwards. Any item still facing backwards after six months should be given away.

After you evaluate your living space and begin shedding possessions take note of how this makes you feel. Minimalism can become quite a positive addiction. Most often scaling down your possessions will leave you with a sense of wholeness instead of a feeling of loss.

NATURE. The next time you feel frazzled or overly stressed, make your way to a patch of woods or, if the weather's bad, find an indoor conservatory and walk (while keeping your mobile phone in your pocket.) While walking practice your deep breathing (inhale for a county of five, hold for five, exhale for a count of five.) The oxygen-rich air and peaceful environment will get to work healing your body and spirit almost immediately. A mindful walk in nature is literally like hitting the reset button for your consciousness and creativity. Using the *Notes* section of this chapter jot down how you feel after you do this.

NOTES

Technology

Focus

Your Stuff

Nature

NOTES

Technology

Focus

Your Stuff

Nature

NOTES

Technology

Focus

Your Stuff

Nature

NOTES

Technology

Focus

Your Stuff

Nature

NOTES

Technology

Focus

Your Stuff

Nature

Chapter Ten

Stress

Short Term Stress-Busters

Sometimes there's no way to escape the stress monster. I refer to it as "the stress monster" because these moments of stress can pop up in our lives at any moment and wreak havoc without warning. No matter how far you advance in your meditation practice, it's impossible to always shield yourself from stressful situations. Stress can occur anywhere: at work; while driving in traffic; when we're immersed in family drama; or experiencing financial problems.

The fastest way to recover from the stress monsters that we haven't prepared for is to be present. What I mean by "being present" is to take your attention away from the memory of the stressful experience that occurred a few seconds or a few minutes in the past and refocus your attention solely and completely on the present moment.

The following are some quick and great ways to quickly be present and find your calm center again.

1. **Conscious Breathing.** Focus all of your attention on your inhalation and your exhalation. Take deep, full inhalations. It's important to feel the belly expand with each breath. Shallow, rapid breathing is unhealthy and a byproduct of stress. Most people adopt a very bad habit of breathing too shallowly all of the time.

2. **Pressure points.** Apply pressure to the side of your index finger with your thumb. If you pay attention to speakers giving presentations you will see them doing this quite often. It's a quick way to calm you during times of high anxiety.

3. **Medulla Massage.** Gently massage the back of your neck at the base of your skull in small circles. This is helpful to relieve current stress as well as the accumulative effects of past stress.

4. **Reconnect with Nature.** A walk in nature has a way of quickly putting things back into their proper perspective.

5. **Simple Physical Activity.** Walk. Cycle. Practice yoga. If you're at work, climb as many stairs as you're able throughout the day and park as far away as your schedule allows.

Long Term Stress-Reducers

Short term stress-busters serve as a sort of triage for stress you've already suffered. Long term stress-reducers are activities that add more joy and satisfaction into your life thereby reducing the negative effects of future stress.

Hobbies

I think of hobbies as a positive and healthy diversions. If you don't already have a hobby, the best way to discover what it should be is ask yourself, "What activities or things am I naturally drawn to?" With the answer to that question, think about ways you can turn it into a hobby. Ideally a hobby should be something you enjoy immersing yourself in so much that when you're doing it you lose track of time.

The most common excuse as to why people don't have hobbies today is lack of time. Ironically, most of us spend hours each day watching television or staring at our mobile devices. It hasn't always been that way. Decades ago, it was very common for people to have one or two real hobbies.

I, for instance, collect vintage watches and have restored (and ride) a vintage English 3-speed bicycle. These hobbies have enhanced my life through what I've learned about them and through connecting with other enthusiasts online who share this same interests. A hobby serves many purposes: it's good for your brain to delve into the minute details of something and it's great for your soul because it provides meaning and purpose. It will even expand your circle of friends by connecting you with other like-minded individuals.

Connect with Nature

When I was a boy, in the nineteen seventies, friends and I would be outside from sun up until sundown. The only time we came inside was for meals.

Gratitude

Remember earlier in the book I explained that in this physical world like attracts like? Recognizing the gifts you already have and being grateful for them not only will make you happier and more satisfied but it will also attract more good things into your life.

Travel

In my opinion traveling and learning about how other people think and live is one of the best educations we can give ourselves. It's very difficult to view someone else as different or hold prejudice beliefs once you truly spend time with them and get to know what makes them tick. I believe humanity needs to do much more of this to realize at our core we're all very much alike.

Continuing Education

Furthering your knowledge could involve anything from adult classes at your community education center to listening to podcasts.

Fun

Do we stop having fun because we age or age because we stop having fun?

I don't know, but one thing is for sure: the world has become far too serious and people don't laugh nearly as much as they used to. Let's change that. Do silly things on a regular basis. Learn a joke and share it, buy a whoopee cushion (whether they admit it or not most everyone thinks farts are funny), swing on a swing, watch live stand-up comedy. Laughter reduces stress, increases your quality of life, and is good for the soul. Animals provide a good example for us, most of them want to play no matter what their age.

NOTES

NOTES

NOTES

NOTES

NOTES

NOTES

Chapter Eleven

Your Meditation Practice

W hat exactly is meditation? It's learning to be completely and wholly present in the moment. It sounds simple, doesn't it?

I guarantee there are a few of you how thought to yourself a few chapters back, *"Okay I've read all these chapters and still haven't learned how to meditate!"* Don't worry, there's a method to my madness. This chapter appears near the end of the book for a reason. If you've made it this far, you have a real interest in trying to integrate the true miracle of meditation into your life. Those who didn't make it this far either didn't connect with the book or weren't ready for the commitment a mindful life requires. These folks will soon be writing a scathing review of this book on Amazon (and that's okay).

Some who've made it this far will put forth a little effort, try meditation half-heartedly for a while, and will quit.

A select few will leap into their meditation practice enthusiastically with both feet. They will experience meditation's many benefits, it will change them, and they will go on to be a proponent of it. They will become a gift to all of us; a positive light that shines as a beacon through the darkness of our world. These are the people for which I wrote this book.

For the benefits of meditation to take root, you must believe in it enough to prepare your life, your soul, your consciousness for this practice. If you do this, meditation will become the calm center that will allow you to weather any storm. This chapter is short but will teach you all you need to know to begin your practice. It's up to you to do the work and practice every single day.

A meditation practice is hard at first, but after a while you will find you look forward to your practice. A little more time will pass and you will find you can't live without it. You will purposely carve time out of your day to practice meditation and when you miss it you will ache for it. Now, let's begin.

Your Space

First and foremost, it helps to have a small area dedicated to meditation practice. This can be a spare bedroom or even a small corner separated with a screen but it should be space that is quiet and with dim light. You should expect your meditation space to be clean, comfortable and free from any unnecessary interruptions or distractions. Many people like to light a candle or burn mild incense but this is not necessary.

It's most beneficial if you meditate in the same space every day. The reason for this is merely occupying this space will evoke calm memories of past meditations. This will allow you to go deeper more quickly and provide a jumpstart to your meditation practice.

Posture

Sit in a comfortable chair with your back straight, shoulders back, and feet flat on the ground. Rest the backs of your hands on the tops your thighs with palms facing upwards.

Preparing Your Body

Just as an athlete stretches before a game before each meditation session it is best to limber yourself up so you don't feel any pain or stiffness during your session and so the energy can flow freely throughout your body. The following exercises will help you achieve a more fruitful meditation experience:

Seated in a chair with your arms straight up in the air reach for the ceiling and elongate your spine. While stretching, rotate your wrists five times and wiggle your fingers for a count of five.

Roll your head slowly and fluidly in one direction five times and then five times in the opposite direction.

Your Practice

There are many styles and types of meditation. The purpose of this book is merely to usher you to the path, to introduce you to the basics. Meditation is just that, practice. These exercises can be done at any time of the day but ideally your meditation routine should be for a few minutes after you wake up and a few minutes just before bedtime.

Ultimately, the important part is to do it, so it is for you to decide how to integrate it into your life. Start with an amount of time that you can devote every day, even if it's five minutes. After you begin to experience how much value this adds to your life, you'll want to gradually lengthen the duration of your practice.

Exercise One - Proper Breathing

This first exercise can be performed seated in a comfortable chair or laying flat on the floor. You should try to keep the spine as straight as possible. I urge you to try this (and only this) exercise for fifteen minutes per day for the first week of your meditation practice. This will give you a proper foundation to build upon.

Bruce Lee said, *"I fear not the man who has practiced ten thousand kicks but I fear the man who has practiced the same kick ten thousand times."*

Mr. Lee realized that by practicing the same simple task again and again, it allows you to eventually perform it perfectly without even thinking about it. I can't stress this enough: proper breathing is the foundation of successful meditation and keeping your consciousness tethered to the present moment.

Let's give it a try:

With eyes closed, inhale through your nose for a slow count of five, hold for a count of five, then exhale through your mouth for a count of five. Breathe slowly and deeply, again inhale for a count of five, exhale for a count of five.

Now, place your open palm on your abdomen. Breathe deeply enough so you can feel your belly rise and fall with each breath.

Concentrate fully on the quality and the fullness of each breath. Repeat this for fifteen minutes per day or longer if you'd like.

This breathing exercise trains the mind to stay in the present moment but it's not always as easy as it seems. Your mind will inevitably try to wander but each time it does acknowledge the thoughts that pop into your head and gently release them. Usher your attention back to your breath.

Not keeping our minds in the here and now is the source of much of the stress in our lives. Living in regret of past mistakes or fear of the future has no value. It only keeps us from experiencing the joy that is happening in our lives right now.

Exercise Two – Psychological/Cleansing

This exercise is best practiced in the seated meditation posture directly after Exercise One.

With eyes closed, place the index finger of your dominant hand directly at the point between your eyebrows. Feel the light pressure of your finger on your forehead and focus your attention directly at this point. Remove your finger but keep your internal attention there. This is where you want to focus your attention during every meditation.

Focus at the point between your eyebrows and imagine your head surrounded by warmth and light. Hold this thought in your imagination for a few moments. Envision this healing light as a bubble that expands with each of your deep exhalations until the light slowly surrounds your whole body.

As you inhale deeply, in your mind's eye, envision the light entering your lungs and gradually permeating every cell in your whole body. Breathe the healing light.

Finally, imagine your whole body glowing. Linger in the warmth and the light with eyes closed, with your attention focused at the point between your eyebrows, concentrating on your long, deep breaths, as long as you're able.

During this exercise, make a mental effort to address any stresses or problems in your life. Feel as though the light is vaporizing them, burning them away. If you have any aches or pains concentrate on the specific body part that needs healing. With several repetitions, mental stress will begin to subside and you will feel more at ease.

Exercise Three – Spiritual/Connecting

Close your eyes and gently focus your eyes to the point between your eyebrows. This will feel a little uncomfortable at first but after a while will seem more natural.

Inevitably your mind will race in rebellion for the mere fact that it's used to being constantly bombarded by stimuli for so many hours of your day. This flood of thoughts is perfectly normal and is your first hurdle on your way to deep meditation. When thoughts come into your mind, don't fight them but acknowledge their presence and simply release them. Let the thoughts go.

Inhale through the mouth for a count of 5
Hold the breath for a count of 5
Exhale through the nose for a count of 5;

again INHALE for 5;
Hold for 5; and
Exhale for 5.

Repeat these as many times as you'd like throughout the day.

These exercises are all you need. Practice them twice per day for a month and you will begin to experience a beautiful and amazing change in your life.

PUTTING IT INTO PRACTICE

Record the progress of your practice in the Notes section of this chapter. List any positive experiences during your practice an any benefits you notice in your life as a result of your practice.

NOTES

NOTES

NOTES

.

NOTES

NOTES

NOTES

Chapter Twelve

It's All About ~~Me~~ WE

"Only a life lived for others is a life worthwhile."

~ ALBERT EINSTEIN

To begin to live a meditation-centered life we must learn to live less for ourselves and more for others. A byproduct of learning to live this way is that you will automatically attract more positive things into your life. When you begin to consciously shift your focus from only yourself to others, an incredible shift begins to happen and you will experience greater abundance.

How many of us know that person who always has to be the center of attention? A person who always steers the conversation in their direction and dominates it. The one who seems a million miles away when you're talking to them. The fact is they're probably not listening at all because they're too busy formulating what they're going to say next. The simple fact is we might, at first, be attracted to the stereotypical alpha personality traits because it seems like they are overflowing with confidence. However, these overly aggressive and narcissistic qualities quickly lose their luster. Eventually most people will make long term connections with those who are good listeners and care about more than just their own wants and needs.

The easiest way to "take a vacation" from yourself and whatever worries you may have is to shift your focus away from "I." Try to empathize with someone who has a different viewpoint than you, and really make an attempt to understand an issue from their point of view. Give of yourself, volunteer for the less fortunate. Pay for a stranger's coffee or anonymously pay for their meal in a restaurant. Alternately, take care of something, buy a houseplant or adopt a pet. These acts of giving will pay you back great dividends of less stress, peace of mind, and higher self-esteem.

When you start paying attention you will see that in life you get what you give. When you're feeling down, the quickest road to recovery is to help someone else out. Also, surround yourself with people who are already like the type of person you're trying to become. Read the biographies of those people who have the traits that you'd like to acquire. Practice being a good listener and you'll be surprised at how many lessons you're missing!

PUTTING IT INTO PRACTICE

Most of us write several e-mails or text messages per day. Pay close attention to how many times you use the words "I" and "me" in your daily correspondence. Also become mindful of how many times you speak the word "I" throughout the course of the day. This is the world's best "self-absorption indicator" and is a little trick that will give you a glimpse of how the rest of the world sees you. Try to consciously reduce the frequency of using the words "me" or "I" in writing and speaking. As a reminder, set a notification on your mobile phone to remind you a couple times per day that, "It's Not All About Me."

Make it a practice to do something nice for someone at least once per day. This can be anything from opening a door, to helping someone change a flat tire, or simply complimenting them on their appearance.

Using the Notes feature of this chapter record how these simple steps make you feel.

NOTES

NOTES

NOTES

NOTES

NOTES

Epilogue

I hope this book sparks a wonderful journey for you. If you've read it to the end, all I can say is I'm honored. If you integrate some of these teachings into your life I will be thrilled. I promise you will not regret it.

50773327R00083

Made in the USA
San Bernardino, CA
03 July 2017